Making Life Happen In the Workplace

Ready Writer Publishing

Copyright

All rights reserved and protected under International Copyright Laws. Any contents of this book including its cover may not be reproduced in whole or in part without the express written permission or consent of the author except in the case of brief quotations embodied in news articles, newsletters, and reviews.

Copyright © 2018 Veronica G. Burnette
All Rights Reserved.

Published by:
Ready Writer Publishing
The United States of America

ISBN: 978-0-9743773-3-9

Veronica G. Burnette
www.veronicatrains.com

Dedication

To all the hard-working individuals who struggle with the demands of everyday work life, I dedicate this to you and your hard work. Without you, the organizations that run the world would not be successful. For every time you were overlooked, undervalued, underpaid, or not openly acknowledged, I applaud you, your efforts, and all the extraordinary work you do. The workforce would be incomplete without you.

Acknowledgments

I want to thank all of the managers and co-workers who inspired me to press past obstacles and endure the challenges we regularly face in the workplace. The lessons learned and wisdom gained through my experiences have caused me to be a better person, trainer, mentor, and coach. Without you I would not be the person I am today.

A special thanks goes to Joss McElroy and Cynthia Harrell for assisting me in the editing process of sharing my wisdom and experiences with the world.

Contents

Introduction 11

It's All About Perspective 19

Let's Talk About It 27

Low and Unfair Pay 35

Lack of Job Security 43

Low Morale 49

Work Relationships 55

Being Micromanaged 61

Lack of Growth & Opportunities 67

Being Overworked 75

Favoritism & Inequality 81

Powerless to Change Anything 87

Conclusion 93

Intelligent people are always ready to learn. Their ears are open for knowledge. (Proverbs 18:15)

Introduction

The word 'work' means "mental or physical activity as a means of earning income". It is a place of employment. Not very many people are born with the privilege of not having to work for their wages. If you are among those who fit this category, I applaud you. Even if you don't have to work, you may still find this resource useful in applying the principles to other areas of your life.

It should go without saying, but for clarification purposes, the definition of a 'workplace' is where people go to render a service. It is a place of production and productivity. Everything else is extra. The benefits of a particular workplace are provisional according to one's needs, which vary from person to person. Despite what we have been led to believe, work is not a chore. It is a privileged obligation. This sounds like an oxymoron, right? How can it be a privilege and an obligation? We need a job to provide for ourselves, but not everyone is privileged to have one. We must understand that having a job and a career is something we not only work toward obtaining but maintaining as well. Therefore, having a job is not only an obligation, it should also be viewed as a privilege. Therefore, it is advisable that we take advantage of every opportunity to learn from every experience within our workplace environment.

Life is meant to be lived and enjoyed, but many people are simply existing rather than living. Employment is a huge part of life as we know it. Why not enjoy it, or at least make the very best of your workplace experiences? On average, we spend 9 hours a day or 40+ hours per week at work. Work becomes our home away from home, so to speak. Other than our families, we spend a great deal of time with those we encounter in the workplace.

You've probably heard the saying, "People do not leave bad companies, they leave bad management." There are many things that cause dissatisfaction in the workplace. According to a Forbes article written in 2018 by Kristi Hedges, the percentage of employees worldwide who find themselves dissatisfied is about 48%. There are more than 80% who feel stressed, and only 30% who feel engaged in and inspired by their careers. There is a plethora of research revealing at the following ten things that are the cause for workplace dissatisfaction:

- Poor communication
- Low or unfair pay
- Lack of job security
- Low morale and unpleasant environment
- Negative relationships with managers and co-workers
- Being micromanaged

- Boredom resulting from lack of growth, recognition, and the opportunity to use skills and abilities
- Feeling overworked and being assigned unrelated job tasks and responsibilities
- Favoritism and inequality
- Feeling powerless to change anything

With so much time and energy spent within the workplace, our jobs often become a vested interest in our lives. Do you work to earn a living, or do you work because you have nothing else better to do? Do you look forward to getting up and going to your place of employment every day? Do you enjoy your job and what you do? Do you get along with your managers and co-workers? If you could change anything about your work life, what would it be? If these questions cause you to have unpleasant thoughts about your job, then the next group of questions will challenge you.

Unless you work from home, the workplace is a huge part of your day. Struggling to get through the day can be stressful, complicated, and at times, unbearable. Although life is full of opportunities, they rarely come knocking on our front door. We must do our best towards making our lives happen and this includes making it happen in the workplace. In order to do that we must be honest with ourselves and face truths. Her are a few questions to ponder. How can you make your work environment more tolerable? What necessary changes are you willing to make? How can you communicate more effectively and get along with managers, co-workers, and others that you encounter regularly? What overall changes do you need to make to become a better employee?

No job is perfect. There will be people, things, and situations that challenge you. Some of these situations and events have caused or will cause you to get upset and become disgruntled, which quite often lead to burnout.

Employment is often viewed as an "**I have to**" area in life. But if we change that way of thinking and develop the mentality of "**I

get to", then work becomes less of a chore and more of an opportunity. These are all teachable moments that create room for growth and maturity. It's all about how you look at your situation. This will require you to change your perspective. This means retraining the way you think and changing your attitude about your workplace. If you are thinking, "I'm completely satisfied with my employment and workplace", then kudos, great and wonderful! Sadly, this is not the case for many.

Changing others is out of our realm of control. However, changing yourselves is quite achievable. Within the workplace, never waste time trying to get others to conform unless you are in some sort of leadership position. Rather, focus your time and energy toward changing yourself. You will then see a change in the way you handle your situations.

You may never change your workplace environments, but you can be transformed by them for the better. This is what is going to make the difference. You will never be held accountable for how you are treated. You will **only** be held accountable for how you respond. Not everyone is financially able to leave their jobs right away. However, you can adopt the necessary mental and emotional skills to cope with the stress that comes with having to deal with difficult situations.

So, what is the key to finding happiness and peace of mind within the workplace? There is no magic wand that will make all your problems go away, but there is a solution. This is a resource tool to help you deal with difficult tasks, personalities, dissatisfaction, and other things that keep you from experiencing joy in the workplace. It is designed to help you change the way you internalize workplace situations.

We will be discussing the ten problem areas of employee dissatisfaction that was previously mentioned. We will focus on solutions that will assist you in navigating your way towards positive outcomes.

*Our thoughts become our beliefs.
Our beliefs become our reality.*

It's All About Perspective
Changing Your Focus

A good leader has the ability to lead, empower, encourage, motivate, and empower those they manage. No leader is better than their team. It is those they manage that get the work done and make them look good. While it is expected that managers, supervisors, or those in leadership positions would and should have these qualities, unfortunately, this is not always the case.

A great deal of expectation is consistently placed on management to keep employees motivated. What better method could there be other than money and recognition? But let's be real. In order to motivate people, they must be willing participants. Without that, no matter what management does, it will not work. It is impossible to motivate those not interested in being motivated. In some cases, there are employees who are comfortable and do not want change. When this is the case, it is unfair to place total responsibility of keeping staff happy or satisfied on management. It is a partnership and there has to be accountability on the part of the employees as well. This is not to say that management is not at all responsible or should not have a hand in keeping good morale in the workplace. We are not playing the blame game. We are simply looking at accountability from both points of view. There are plenty of awesome managers in the world who are excellent advocates for their employees. Management would be easy if everyone were manageable. However, if employees have gotten comfortable with being comfortable, there is not much anyone can do to encourage them to do better or be more productive. To be frank, some people are easy to manage, while others can be quite difficult. Therefore, employees must **own** their part and take responsibility as well.

So, what about those good and exceptional employees who fall victim to becoming frustrated due to an unpleasant work environment under poor management? It is a wonderful thing when companies have policies and procedures in place aimed to maximize performance through motivational incentives and techniques. In a perfect world, this would be every company's method in obtaining and maintaining positive employee morale. Keep in mind that humans are running these organizations. When dealing with humans, you get an assortment of personalities with different leadership styles.

In dealing with humans, we know there are good people who manage, but that does not make them good managers. So, from an employee's perspective, what can be done to survive under those who are not equipped to lead and manage? How does one survive in their work environment and make the best of their workplace experiences?

It is a known fact that circumstances and environments shape our lives and the way we think, function, and process information. Every company has its own culture and way of doing things. There used to be a time when a company would hire a person based on their skills. Now, companies are not only looking at your skills and experience, they are also looking to see how you fit within their culture. They are looking to see how well you will get along with the different personalities already employed. Take a look at the 50 most common interview questions. You will find a few questions that are designed to understand your ability to adjust to the culture of that organization.

Here are a few examples:

- Tell me about a challenge or conflict you've faced at work and how you dealt with it.

- What type of work environment do you prefer?
- How would your boss and co-workers describe you?
- How do you deal with pressure or stressful situations?
- What are your pet peeves at work?

One of the most common mistakes employees make is expecting their workplace environments to become conducive to them. In actuality, they need to make the necessary adjustments to function well at the workplace.

Changing your focus to include the way you internalize situations, the way you process information, and the way you perceive your condition, empowers you to make better choices. Changing your focus also helps to alleviate the dread of doing things you find unpleasant. When you look at the "**doing**" as an opportunity, it will diminish the mental and emotional stress that comes with the "**having to**." Rather than looking at the fact that you **"have to"** go to work, change that ideology to **"I get to"** go to work. This shifts and changes the dreaded chore into a mental opportunity. This simple act of turning a negative into a positive allows you to see it from a different perspective.

Here is another example. Retraining your mind by saying "I get to go to work because having a job allows me to take care of myself and my family. I get to go to work because it allows me to pay my bills. I get to go to work because having a job allows me to have nice things and live comfortably. I get to because having a job also allows me to gain experience and move forward. I get to because ..." (you finish this sentence).

This line of thinking can be applied to every area of your life. When we change the way we think, we change our lives. Your life is governed by your internal filter. What is your internal filter? I'm glad you asked. Your internal filter is your heart. There is a Christian proverb that states, "As a man thinks in his heart, so is he." In other words, the condition of your heart governs your life. It is the filter that everything concerning your life passes through. Therefore, if your heart is broken, you will see through broken-hearted lenses. When we are hurt, bitter, angry, or expecting rejection, judgement, or some type of other negative response, we often become defensive and respond accordingly.

Our life right now is a culmination of the decisions we have made up to this point. Those decisions were most likely influenced by the condition of our hearts at the time we made them. In order to get better results, we must learn to make better decisions.

*You are not held accountable
for how you are treated.
You are accountable for how you respond.*

Let's Talk About It
The Need for Effective Communication

Communication means the impartation and exchange of information or news. Communicating is more than just talking. One of the most powerful benefits of effective communication in the workplace is effective interaction among employees and managers. Individuals are more engaged in their work and can better align with company objectives and goals when the foundation of its culture is built on the way communication is established in teams and workplace environments. The downside is when the wrong type of information or communication is exchanged or the perception of what is being communicated is misinterpreted. This creates an atmosphere of contention and distrust that disrupts workspace. It can cripple an organizational environment and have a negative impact and consequences on the entire staff.

Understand that everyone does not speak the same language when it comes to the way we communicate. You may be an introvert trying to function in an extroverted environment or vice versa. While some are comfortable with more involvement, there are those who are turned off or bothered by too much interaction. It is a good idea to get to know yourself and your co-workers by understanding the different personality types you all have. Taking a personality test and having a team-building discussion is a fun way to get to know yourself and your co-workers. There are quite a few free online tests. Work together with your co-worker and decide on which one you will take together.

Learning to detect poor communication habits and replace them with positive ones will require some personal introspective work along with a willingness to listen, receive and make the necessary changes. There are three main ways we typically communicate with one another. Let's take a look at each of them:

Nonverbal communication includes facial expressions, eye contact, gestures, posture, body language, and even touch; they are wordless signals that speak volumes.

Quite a bit can be read into gestures, facial expressions, and body language. This is a highly misunderstood form of nonverbal communication. It has caused many assumptions to be made. Because of these assumptions, it creates negative vibes and tension between individuals, especially in the work environment. Something as simple as the folding of the arms while speaking can give the impression that a person is angry when, in actuality, they could be cold. Folding or holding their arms could also be a comfortable posture. For this reason, it is a good practice to not make assumptions about others.

Written communication includes emails, notes, letters, texts, instant messaging, or any type of information transmitted to a written or typed format.

In a world where emojis and text language are becoming the normal way to communicate, we have to be careful how our written communication is being relayed. How many times have you sent a message that caused conflict because of the way it was interpreted? So much can be read into it depending on the recipient.

It is important to be mindful and careful of the tone of the words being used to relay the information. Try choosing words that will not be viewed as threatening or offensive. For example, words typed in all caps are viewed as yelling or being angry. You've probably heard "Please and thank you go a long way." These are two powerful words that can soften the tone of any message.

There is no room in the workplace for acronyms, such as those used when sending personal text messages. Within a professional environment, you want to display professionalism at all times and represent yourself as a person with integrity.

Oral communication is transmitted through the avenue of speech. Therefore, it is important to be conscious of vocal tones and facial expressions.

We all learn and process information differently. Therefore, we should never assume another person understands what or how we are thinking. The more information you provide to help the individual understand what you are trying to say, the better. An important thing to remember about the way we communicate is less is not always better. As a matter of fact, less communication creates more problems when not enough information is shared.

In every situation, it is important to take the necessary steps to explain what is being communicated as if the person is hearing it for the first time. Then have a dialogue about what is being communicated so that all parties understand and are fully aware of what is being discussed. It may sound elementary or unnecessary, but again, it cuts down on the confusion that could later result in problems due to a lack of information or lack of communication.

It is always a good idea to have checks and balances in place. This is to cover yourself and keep the lines of communication open and clear. Having checks and balances means having a backup plan just in case there is some type of disconnect that causes miscommunication. This starts with sending a written notification when possible, perhaps in e-mail or text message, where it can be retrieved if necessary. However, before sending it, you will want to make sure the tone of the message is professional and courteous.

Some individuals may see this as being too over the top or petty. But it is your record of what and when information is being communicated. It cuts down on misunderstandings because you never know when a situation might come back to bite you.

These are just a few tips to use as a way to stay ahead of communication issues or lack thereof. You will save quite a bit of headaches if you work from the mindset of being proactive rather than reactive.

Do not expect others to value in you what you do not value in yourself. Know your worth.

Low and Unfair Pay
How Much Is It Worth to You?

There are two choices in life when it comes to paying your bills: you can either work to earn a paycheck or depend on the kindness of others. Most responsible adults learn and apply the necessary principles to maintain self-sufficiency. That means working and earning a living. Nowadays, even children and teens are becoming self-sufficient by becoming millionaires as early as ages 12 and 13. However, many of us did not recognize or feel the pressure of needing to work until reaching the legal age of adulthood. We all have to start somewhere. So, we accepted our first job, perhaps at a fast-food restaurant, grocery store, shopping mall, or some other job that did not require experience or much skill. We worked for low pay. All of that is good for those who have no responsibilities that require ends to meet. But for those who are working to earn the necessary money to pay bills and sustain a comfortable lifestyle, earning minimum wage is not the answer.

One of the top ten reasons many are frustrated with their career or workplace is because of low or unfair pay. Obtaining a job does not guarantee you will get the money that's needed to pay your bills. This makes the continued search for adequate employment necessary. However, looking for a job becomes a job in itself.

During the process of having to search for work, many feel the pressure or urgency to accept a position that may not be ideal. Many become comfortable with the safety of having employment and cease to continue searching.

Let's be honest. Who does not like getting more than what they are paying for?

Unfortunately, this is how many organizations and their management teams work. If they can get more out of you for less pay, they will. But the goal is not to allow anyone to take advantage of you. Don't allow this to discourage you because there are some fair-minded employers. However, this is not found across the board. Therefore, the questions are: Do you know your worth? Are you getting paid what you deserve based on your knowledge and experience? If your answer is no, then it is time to do something different.

Low and unfair pay is one of the leading causes of many employees being disgruntled about their jobs. This often leads to low or no work performance, which creates another set of problems. If you are not getting paid, why try, right? Without even trying, displaying that frustration begins to show openly. The question then becomes, "How can this be fixed?" Understanding your options and what is available to you is the first step toward success.

Ask your employer for a raise. Before approaching your manager, here are some things to consider: You will want to research salary data. Make sure the timing of your approach is right. Be realistic when asking and have proper documentation to back up how much you are asking for and why. There is an art to negotiating your salary. If you are not comfortable asking, get advice on how to become more confident. You may very well get a "No". Don't get discouraged. If it is important to you, fight for it. If you believe it belongs to you, then take the necessary time, strategize, and make plans to revisit the subject.

Keep a detailed record of your daily job tasks and responsibilities. Compare this to your current job description. If the two do not match and you find yourself performing above and beyond, use this as leverage to ask for a raise.

Stay up to date with your knowledge and skills. Be more visible by asking your managers to consider you for additional duties. This will provide an opportunity to increase your knowledge and skill level. Identify projects and events, then offer your time, talent, and skills. Reach out to co-workers and help them with their work assignments when you see an opportunity, even if it is not your direct responsibility. This may allow you to learn additional skills that you are not able to obtain within your current role. What you are showing managers is that you are willing and dependable. It will look good on performance reviews, and potentially put you in the running for bonuses and pay increases.

If you are striving for longevity with the company you are currently working with, seeking higher-paid positions within the company is another way to get the financial increase you desire. This may require additional skills and education. Many companies have programs that will pay for school or provide tuition reimbursement for their employees to further their education. Do your research. You may be pleasantly surprised at what you find.

One of the issues with many frustrated employees is their lack of knowledge and understanding of the rights and benefits offered to them. When you are first employed on a job, it is a good idea to read the employee manual which explains the company's policies and procedures, along with all the employee rights and benefits. Many are blinded by the excitement of obtaining the job, they fail to investigate any further.

While you are working on your education, you may want to do some volunteering to obtain the skills you will need. Once you have obtained both the education and skills, you will be equipped to advance to a higher paying position. Don't box yourself in. The position you seek may not be with your current employer. Look for positions within sister companies. It is understandable, however, if you desire to stay within a certain umbrella that multiple companies are under. It is understandable to want to build longevity, as there are certain benefits such as pension and retirement along with many others. Do your research, as there are ways to transfer from company to company without losing your benefits.

Having higher pay is always a win-win. Not only does it boost your confidence and morale, it also causes you to have a greater appreciation for your job and career. If you are not satisfied with your current rate of pay, the approaches listed in this section are just a few things to consider that may help you change that. Don't get frustrated, get busy.

*There will always be those who
Do not value your worth.
Don't allow yourself to be one of them!*

Lack of Job Security
What's In It for Me?

In an ideal world, finding a good-paying job that will last until retirement would be the golden employment ticket. Unfortunately, this type of job has become a thing of the past. Living with the uncertainty of job security is quite daunting. It causes individuals to become overwhelmed with fear of the unknown, followed by anxiety and stress.

Safety is a psychological need for every human, according to Maslow's Hierarchy of Needs, "A Theory of Human Motivation" by Abraham Maslow. Financial security is one requirement of being safe. Although many are not satisfied with their workplace, the security of having a steady income makes it tolerable. The lack of finances affects every area of an individual's life. It is true that money can't buy happiness, but it can definitely be a major ingredient for making life happen.

The workplace is a major investment for many. Employees perform better when they feel secure in their environment. Many companies' approach to innovation means an increase in turnover due to the increased rate of technological evolution. More and more employees are being replaced or their jobs are being outsourced. The writing has been on the wall for many years. Unfortunately, more and more companies are forced to downsize or completely shut their doors altogether.

When faced with this kind of uncertainty, what can be done? Knowing your rights as an employee cannot be stressed enough. Do your research and see what that company has to offer as far as prospective advancement. Is the current position you're in a dead end? Does the position you are about to accept have opportunity for advancement? These are questions you must ask yourself. This is also where the employee manual becomes extremely important. In it you will get the "inside scoop".

Have a conversation about job security concerns with your supervisor/manager if and when you feel comfortable doing so. This may help alleviate any worries and answer the important questions. It is important to NEVER let your guard down becoming comfortable and complacent in any position. Understand your worth and keep yourself valuable by staying "skilled up". Always be in a "seeking to advance" frame of mind. In other words, always look for ways to grow; develop and improve your skills, talents, and abilities because longevity is no longer a guarantee.

Many individuals tend to wait until they need a resume before making revisions. Take nothing for granted. Keep your resume and portfolio up to date. If you do not have a portfolio, it would be wise to develop one. It is an excellent way to showcase your skills, work performed, volunteerism, special projects, publications, education, awards, letters of recommendation, and other professional accomplishments that will impress employers.

Take advantage of professional development training courses. Stay up to date on your certifications and other classes that will help you keep up with technological industry changes. Make sure to keep your manager or supervisor well informed of what you are doing. When opportunities come or when subject matter experts are needed for projects, you will be in the running.

This can be a touchy subject for some, but budgeting and saving money is always a good idea under all circumstances. When dealing with job insecurity, it is important to be prepared for the what-ifs. Life happens and when it does, having a cushion allows you to have something to fall back on. It will alleviate stress and give you time to look and prepare for the next set of opportunities.

You've probably heard the phrase, "When one door closes, another one opens." Instead of worrying about possible job loss, think of it as an opportunity to not simply **go on**, but to **grow on** and do better things. Sometimes, we have to be pushed out of our places of comfort. When that happens, we are forced to move beyond our fears. This is where dreams become reality. In order to obtain something you've never had, this means doing something you've never done. Change is not all bad; in fact, it's often necessary. Learning to embrace it can make life much easier.

No one can make you feel inferior without your permission.

Low Morale

"When They Go Low, You Go High"

Morale is defined as an individual's level of psychological well-being based on a sense of purpose and self-confidence. Even the most confident, skilled, and highly educated individual may find themselves feeling as if they are taken for granted, unappreciated, overworked, underpaid, overlooked, scrutinized, and a number of things that cause tension and grief in the workplace. Many of these frustrated places are being discussed throughout this book, along with the art of learning ways to deal with them.

From a managerial perspective, there are several things that can be done to improve morale, such as:

- Acknowledging employees and thanking them for doing well.
- Have regular meetings that include team building and empowerment sessions to help employees de-stress and feel appreciated.
- Be approachable and inviting so that employees feel they can speak with you about work-related issues.
- Be open to change and taking the necessary steps to create and maintain a stress-free environment. Studies show increased productivity results from having a stress-free workplace environment.

Confidential surveys are excellent ways to obtain feedback from employees, especially those who feel they cannot speak freely or fearful of speaking openly.

When you know the morale is low, it is important to find something that helps you stay focused on things that will keep you motivated. Many initiatives are focused on how to boost employee morale from the leadership's perspective as stated previously. Although that is good, we want to also identify what can be done from the employee's perspective as well.

First things first, morale as an employee is ultimately dependent on you as the individual. Don't wait for anyone to make you feel better. You get to control how you feel. Everything starts with a decision. Relatively speaking, no one can make you feel low unless you allow them to do so. One of the most valuable lessons learned from **experiencing low morale** is understanding what not to do. It is the golden rule that says, "Do unto others as you would have them do unto you."

Believe it or not, the little things you do go a long way. Greeting your co-workers with a smile and a hearty "Good morning" lightens the mood in a room. Whether you get the response you want or not, keep shining and being brilliant. Over time, the atmosphere and the way some individuals respond to you will change.

Sometimes low morale happens because people do not feel as if they are being heard. Take the time to ask your co-workers about their day. Keep it light and general without getting personal. Too much information can often become a snare. Do for your co-workers things you would want them to do for you. Their responses may not be reciprocated, but do it anyway. You never know what impact you are making and the lives you are changing.

Remember, it's all about perspective and how you choose to handle situations. Will you have moments? Absolutely! But the key is not allowing those moments to have you. Will you have negative experiences? Yes, but learn to make the best of every workplace experience whether good or bad. As stated before, you may not be able to change the culture within the environment, but you do have control over how you respond to that culture.

As Michelle Obama stated, "When they go low, we go high." In other words, when people and situations try to hinder or take you down, you do everything you can to keep your head up and rise above the situation. It is not impossible. It simply requires a little self-motivation. Your mission, should you choose to accept it, is to find your mental and emotional happy place. This will be your mental and emotional outlet and place of escape when people and situations come to challenge you.

Here is an additional tip: Never be afraid of challenges. Embrace them because every challenge is not designed to cripple or destroy you. Many of them actually inspire great productivity. It will push you into places you never thought you'd be.

Everyone does not deserve the title "Friend"

Work Relationships
Friend or Frenemy

Many relationships are formed and established through day-to-day interactions with co-workers. These relationships are not like those we establish with casual or social acquaintances. When you think about relationships with family and friends, these are more intimate in nature. There is a bond of closeness where you are free to let your hair down. In the workplace, this may not be a good idea. You will want to have personal and professional boundaries in place that will safeguard you as an employee with workplace relationships. It is necessary to guard yourself by not allowing too much of you to show because there will be those who may misinterpret who you are, or they won't be able to handle and appreciate the real you.

Our workplace relationships are not like our other relationships, based on the fact that they are imposed upon us, so to speak. This is because we do not get to choose who the company decides to hire to work alongside us. In this case, we must learn to accept the good with the bad. This is not to say that all relationships in the workplace are bad. But let's face it—all are not ideal either.

The workplace is an excellent place to network and connect. If you acquire a few friends that you can interact with outside of your place of employment, that is great. However, this is not the intent for most when accepting employment. You are at your job to perform a service and do what you are being paid to do. Unfortunately, many individuals lose sight of this and find themselves caught up in conflicts, not understanding where to draw the line.

Part of making life happen in the workplace is enjoying your co-workers, but not getting caught up in the drama that often comes with too much togetherness. For mature professionals, this should never be the case; but unfortunately, it happens.

Every relationship has its own set of challenges, and workplace relationships can be particularly challenging especially when lines become blurred. This often happens with bosses and those they supervise. They may find themselves wanting to be their employees' friend one day, then switch to putting on their manager's hat when it comes time to be a supervisor. This is difficult when it is time for employee evaluations. When their employee, who is also their friend, scores less than perfect on their performance evaluation, it creates a problem. This sends mixed signals that will ultimately cause a rift in the personal relationship. On the other hand, when an employee, who is also the manager's friend, is shown favoritism and their flaws are overlooked at the expense of other employees, that too, becomes a problem.

What can you do when the lines of a relationship become blurred? It is helpful to have a conversation and communicate how you feel. During that conversation, you will need to be open and honest while establishing new boundaries. It may be emotionally challenging because it will undoubtedly change the dynamics of the relationship. This is a conversation that becomes necessary in order to maintain a pleasant workplace environment. This is just one example. Throughout your experiences, you've probably encountered a few more.

The manager/employee is not the only relationship that could make life at work difficult. There are also the typical relationships that are developed between co-workers. They often start off good, but frustration due to many things can destroy them, causing the work environment to no longer be pleasant.

As a rule, do not divulge any information you do not want to be leaked, shared, or repeated. Everyone does not have your best interest at heart. You may have a wonderful working relationship with your co-workers. However, that does not make them your friends. Think back to a time when your personal interactions have caused unpleasant situations in the workplace. Unfortunately, sharing too much information can, and in some cases, will be used against you. Keep everything on a professional level and monitor personal involvements. This is nothing new. Look at past encounters and govern yourself accordingly moving forward. As stated before in the section on effective communication, it is much easier to be proactive than reactive. You may not get to choose who is hired for you to work with, but you do get to practice discretion and exercise professionalism within your workplace relationships.

Being a good person is not a qualification for being a good manager.

Being Micromanaged
Under Constant Surveillance

There is nothing more frustrating for a person with experience than to be micromanaged. "I need to be scrutinized, consistently watched, and made to feel incompetent", says NO ONE ever! Even those who are considered novices would get a little perturbed by constantly having their shoulders looked over.

The act of being micromanaged indicates to employees they are not trustworthy, dependable, or intelligent enough to complete tasks and assignments. If you were hired to do a job, you should be given the freedom to do what you were hired to do, right? That depends on the style of leadership of your manager. When you first accept a position, you are only given a glimpse into the type of people you will have the privilege of working with. It is not until you spend a few days or perhaps weeks that you get a full picture of what your work life will be like within that organization. You may not be used to being monitored as closely as a micromanager tends to do. You may not be in a position to leave your job right away. Until the day comes that you are able to transfer or leave altogether, you will have to make some extreme adjustments. This can be painful, but it will cause you to adopt new mental skills of endurance. So, this is not altogether, a bad thing.

Here are some other things to consider: Your manager may be feeling pressured by their management. Do not take it personally. Do not allow first impressions to be your only impression. Never assume they are egotistical or unfair individuals. Get to know the manager(s) better before passing judgment. It may not be them at all. It may simply be the culture of the organization. When a period of time has passed and their personality presents itself to be one that is difficult to work with and one that is controlling in nature, then adjust yourself accordingly. Even if you have no respect for the person, it is important to respect their position.

Those who are micromanagers tend to have control issues. Things are going to be their way or no way. The irony is they do not like the idea of being controlled. If you have never worked with or encountered this type of personality, here is an excellent opportunity to learn. Learning is not always about understanding what to do correctly. Much of what you will learn from a micromanager is what **not** to do in your role as a manager or supervisor. Experience is the best teacher. Once you have adapted and learned additional skills, they will undoubtedly help you further your career.

Here are some steps you can take when dealing with being micromanaged. The first and most important thing is to relax and find your happy place. Being frustrated will only make matters worse. There is no point in fighting back. Your heightened energy is only fuel that will provoke and escalate the situation.

Remember as previously discussed, you do not **"have to"** you **"get to."** So, do it with a good attitude and a smile. Don't allow others to see how they get to you. Not to say they are purposely trying to frustrate you. But if in fact you truly are working with someone who takes pleasure in seeing how far they can control you, it will only give them a reason to apply additional pressure if you resist. Choose your debates and pick your battles. Remember they are in a position that could very well determine whether you stay or go. Because of their controlling nature, you will want to keep them in the loop by keeping them up to date about what you are doing and how you are progressing. Keep paper trails by sending frequent emails letting them know your progress. This might seem a little excessive, but it is a good practice to incorporate in any position. It protects you in a variety of ways. Because a micromanager likes to have his/her hands in everything, they get overwhelmed and forgetful at times. Keeping documentation of things you've notified them about, have already done, and are doing is the best way to protect yourself.

Offer your assistance to lighten their load. By doing this and keeping them in the loop, you are also creating a pattern of trust. At some point, they may let their guard down and allow you more autonomy without so much of their input. If you really feel the need to let them know how you feel, wait for the appropriate time. Gather your thoughts and rehearse your plan of action. Give them a chance before approaching a higher authority. If this does not work, make sure to follow the chain of command along with company policy and procedures regarding filing grievances. Hopefully, it will not get to this point. But if it does, you will want to keep excellent documentation of this as well.

The only person that has the power to stop you from growing is you.

Lack of Growth & Opportunities
Nowhere Else to Grow

Imagine being a bird in a case with handcuffs on. This poor bird is being hindered from doing what it has been created to do. This creature is born to FLY. This is how it feels to be locked into a position without being given the freedom to grow and function in what you as an employee know how to do. Where there is no outlet, lack of growth and opportunity to expand and grow, the job becomes mundane, routine, and quite frankly— BORING! It is a known fact, that when employees become bored and are no longer interested in their job duties, the quality of their performance becomes somewhat less than usual. Employee performance becomes robotic and then they are simply going through the motions of getting through their day. It can be a place of extreme frustration. So, what can be done?

Speak with your manager, especially during the time of performance review and come up with a plan. This is not only an opportunity for them to give you their feedback and expectations regarding your performance, it is also a time for you to speak up about your performance. Let your aspirations and desires be known moving forward, along with your expectations. Performance reviews are usually given around the same time every year. Therefore, you already have an idea of when to expect one. With this information in tow, you have time to make some realistic decisions and come up with a written plan to present at your review. Most professionals respond better to written documentation. It is highly recommended that you always use this as part of your communication efforts any time you have to represent yourself professionally. Over time, if there is no change, it may be time to do something different and move on. It may very well mean that you have outgrown the position and/or the company.

As stated previously, looking for employment is a job within itself. That can also become a place of contention. While you wait, you have to fight through the feelings of being stuck in a position where you no longer feel valued. Until you are able to transition into your next place of employment, learning to channel those feelings of despair and frustration is key. Consider the following:

A playground is defined as a place, environment, facility, or area used for recreation, play, and exercise. A playground is where you can expect to see children laughing, playing, fighting, crying, and learning to successfully navigate and function within the great big world around them. The playground also helps children get rid of their pent-up energy. Such energy, if not released, might otherwise cause frustration and stunt their growth process. Some of the best life lessons are learned during childhood. The playground is an extremely important place because children need a safe place to play.

In the world of Information Technology (IT), new programs are being developed daily. When learning a new program, there is an area within the program referred to as "the playground" or the "sandbox." Ironically, the sandbox is often found on the playground. Within the program, this is the place where trainees practice. They play around while learning what to do. They also learn what not to do. It is the place of growth and development. They are designated areas where a lesson is learned from the mistakes being made. It is a safe place to learn how to function before, what the IT world calls, "going live." Once the trainee goes "live", they are no longer in training. They have been released to perform within a new level of authority. This is the place the trained individual now has the power to make life-changing decisions. It is vitally important for them to be properly developed and skillfully matured before being released into active duty.

Merry-go-rounds, swing sets, teeter-totters, monkey bars, and sandboxes are all types of equipment found on the playground. They are recreational equipment infants and toddlers use for play. In becoming adults, we typically move on to more mature things that pertain to life and living it. There are lessons learned during times of immaturity that are strategically instrumental to our development. With many of the positions we desire to occupy, we may not be quite ready, as they require levels of maturity beyond where we are right now. In order to advance to the next level, we must remain on the playground and sandboxes of our current situation. During this time of adjustment, it helps to recognize our preparedness through the mistakes we make. Our attitude and responses to these mistakes and being corrected is a true test of character.

This may not be your place of flight. If the opportunity presents itself, GREAT! If it does not, remember to not allow yourself to get frustrated by it. Change your focus and internalize it differently. Look at this position as your sandbox on the playground. It is the place where you learn the necessary things before going live in your next place called "There".

The playground is instrumental in helping children develop their people skills. In other words, they learn to "play nice" and get along with others. Because of some professionally unfortified places, these abrasive workplace situations are helping you to develop and grow. You are learning to build your endurance muscles.

When we do not learn from our mistakes, we tend to repeat them. Don't despise your training places. Seek out the silver linings and the lessons they teach. Ask yourself these questions: What lesson can I learn from this place of discomfort? What am I being groomed for? How can I use this experience to my advantage to better myself?

As it was stated at the beginning of this book, until the pain of staying the same outweighs the pain to change, we normally don't. Sometimes the pressure that is applied through our situations is the very thing that propels us into our greatest purpose.

Embrace your challenges. They will push you into places you never thought you would be.

Being Overworked
Say "When"

Burnout is a real thing. It results from emotional, physical, and mental exhaustion caused by excessive and prolonged stress. The concept of being overworked is relative to the individual. For the population of workaholics who are driven by having a seemingly unending workload—no problem. Not having a social life may be quite normal for them. But for the rest of the working class, they would probably tell you that being overworked is not okay.

As you can see from the above definition, stress-related burnout is a real issue. Even those areas of passion can become places of stress and frustration when employees find themselves overworked. Those passions will no longer be enjoyable resulting in slow to no productivity.

A company's goal is always to increase the bottom-line figure. If they are not driven by dollar signs, they are driven by numbers that, in turn, lead them to increased revenue. For this reason, there are quite a few reasons individuals find themselves overworked due to no fault of their own. Being overworked is often a side effect of being dependable. You've heard it said that good help is hard to find.

When managers find those who are dependable, the ones they know can be counted on to get the job done and reach their organizational goals, they place a large amount of responsibility on these individuals and often overlook the fact that these employees may be suffering under the weight of the responsibilities they have been given. Employees may find themselves compelled to keep silent for fear of not wanting to appear weak, incompetent, or a number of other reasons.

This, in turn, creates a stressful environment that will eventually lead to burnout if not dealt with appropriately.

Another ingredient for being overworked is when relative job duties, assigned tasks and responsibilities related to employee job descriptions are not taken into consideration by supervisors and managers. It is all about getting the job done and, unfortunately, those dependable employees will find themselves becoming overwhelmed when given the tasks and responsibilities of their co-workers that are underperforming.

One of the questions to ask yourself is "Am I really being overworked, or am I dissatisfied in other areas that cause me to think and feel as if I'm being overworked?" For instance, lack of job security, inequality, lack of growth and adequate pay, or some of the other reasons listed in this book. Let's face it—being overworked does not seem as daunting when the pay matches the expectation of the workload.

If you are truly being overworked unfairly, these are a few tips. Speak to co-workers in an effort to work together and come up with an equal and fair system for getting tasks done. You will want to do this before going to the next level. One thing about management, if at all possible, they want to see employees work together and find solutions before approaching them with problems.

Create for yourself a job responsibility and timeline journal to keep a record of tasks that you are assigned and perform daily. This will be proof of how much work you are doing. Without some type of documentation, it may appear that you are simply complaining and not wanting to do the work. Remember to always cover yourself with documentation.

Journal enough information to gather adequate evidence, then schedule a meeting with management to discuss your concerns. Be patient, you may have to meet with them more than once to show a progression or pattern. In cases where you have to explain why projects are incomplete or deadlines are missed, this timeline journal will show the demands of your workload.

Always take a look at your situation from both angles. If being overworked is a result of poor time management, keeping a log of what you do will also help you determine if you need to shift, refocus, and do away with whatever is stealing your productivity time.

A part of making life happen in the workplace is being able to enjoy the rest of your life when you exit the workplace. If you find that these and other things you've tried have not worked and things are not getting better, it is time to look for an exit. Your physical, mental, and emotional health matters.

Dissatisfaction is a tool that consistently pushes you toward purpose.

Favoritism & Inequality
It's All In Who You Know

No one likes being a victim of inequality or favoritism, especially when it affects their livelihood. Favoritism is:

- watching others breeze by and get promoted over those who are clearly more qualified for the position.
- having to report to an individual who was once your co-worker, but has now become your manager without merit.
- having to train someone to understand their role and responsibility who has been promoted over you.
- watching someone being put in charge of projects they clearly know nothing about, while depending on your

expertise to get it done, but you never receive any credit or recognition.
- watching individuals consistently move up in rank above other employees who possess years of experience and more education.
- seeing co-workers being promoted or given positions without having to go through the application process.
- seeing others get away with noncompliance or breaking rules for which others have previously been terminated.

Does any of this sound familiar? If so, you may be the victim of favoritism and inequality. "It's all about who you know" is the golden rule of favoritism. Unfortunately, depending on the mindset of the ones in charge, no matter how competent, efficient, or experienced you are, those qualities alone are not enough to get you promoted. Why? Because favoritism happens when relationships between employees and their managers go beyond the workplace. Discrimination in any form breeds favoritism and inequality.

Think about your family member, best friend, or even those you have a very strong like for in the workplace. Wouldn't you want the best for them? It is human nature to cater to what we like and hold at bay or reject people and things we do not care about. This is how discrimination and favoritism works. Unfortunately, if managers know they can get away with it, they will push that envelope. Could it be that it is also about control? The one doing the favoring gets to decide who, what, when, and how much. Is it unfair? Absolutely! But haven't you heard that favor isn't fair? Let's be honest. If you were the one in the position of being favored, you most likely will have little to no complaints about being there. We typically complain when there is no gain. Therefore, we will look at it from both perspectives.

Imagine how your co-workers feel when they are in the position of being overlooked and given all the crappy grunge work. They are looking at you with disdain because the boss has favored and promoted you to places you did not earn on your own. Now internalize their pains of frustration and adjust your sail. This will help you not to become what you dislike.

If you are a victim of inequality in the workplace, your first line of defense is to document, document, **DOCUMENT**! This cannot be stressed enough. Once you have enough proof and want to pursue some form of action, you must first get to know your organization's policy and procedures. Some companies have regulations regarding nepotism. The definition of nepotism is the practice among those with power or influence of favoring relatives or friends, especially by giving them jobs. As favoritism in the workplace can be a form of discrimination, this then becomes a legal issue. However, the burden of proof is on the part of the plaintiff. This is where documentation will be your best friend. Never rely on co-workers to come to your defense, as they may be afraid to speak up due to fear of retaliation.

When dealing with people, this behavior has become somewhat acceptable, especially in the private sectors that are governed by their own set of guidelines and bylaws. If you are working for the government or state entity, you may have options. Weigh your options before you decide to expose inequality. By bringing it to the attention of your manager's boss or the human resources department, you may be subjecting yourself to additional negative behaviors. Retaliation is a real thing and it happens even in the subtlest of ways. This is something to evaluate when deciding what course of action you plan to take. Always think before you act. Seek wise, unbiased counsel, then prepare and safeguard yourself. Without documented proof, your grievance may not be taken seriously. It will simply be your word against theirs. Make sure to follow the chain of command so it will not be used against you and hold up the process.

*You may be powerless to change your situation. You are **not** powerless in determining how it changes you.*

Powerless to Change Anything
Why Try?

During the interview, a potential employee is only given a snapshot of the position they will occupy. They energetically pursue with passion, full of hope and ideas. This, after all, is what they have been training for and are now positioned to let their light shine—so they thought. This is an all too familiar place for many.

New employees never truly know what they are getting themselves into or how they are going to feel about a position and the work environment until they've had an opportunity to get their feet wet. Once they become acclimated, it is never too early to set new goals or see themselves moving and advancing, even if it means transferring to a new position or finding employment with a different company altogether.

There used to be a time when staying in one position for a long period of time was favorable. This is no longer the case. If a person has not advanced within five years, it is viewed by some employers as being stagnant or complacent. To a potential employer, it might signal a red flag. Longevity, in this case, makes it appear that the individual has not done anything to enhance their knowledge and skills. It is important to keep increasing and improving skill sets. In doing so, employees are able to show progression even within the same position. When progression and efforts toward improvement that bring about departmental or organizational change for the better are met with resistance, what can be done?

When dealing with feelings of being powerless to change anything, more than likely it's because employee efforts are consistently being rejected or met with unwilling challenges on the part of management. Employees with driver personality types are problem solvers who want to implement change. They consistently seek ways to improve and become greater assets within their positions. But when they are not given the opportunity to be the change agents they are meant and often hired to be, they reach breaking points where passion and zeal will dwindle. Here are a few things you might want to try.

When you are driven with a supportive personality, it is difficult to stand by and watch someone or something fail especially when you know you can do something to change the outcome. Your knee-jerk reaction is to jump in and assist. However, don't be so eager to show how much you know by giving solutions to every problem. Nobody likes a "know-it-all". And don't give away all your secrets. You will only come across as pushy, egotistical, or arrogant. Allow your manager to approach you for solutions.

Present your ideas and be willing to step back and be okay if they are not accepted. You've probably heard it said "I can show you better than I can tell you." Showing rather than telling should be your next course of action. Failure typically causes people to rethink their approach to solving problems. This may open the door for your ideas to be incorporated.

Someone is always watching, so be patient and supportive even when you are not in the driver's seat. Never give up! Your ideas matter. You were given these abilities for a reason. You are **NOT** powerless when it comes to making changes. Your powerlessness is only limited to your position, not your condition.

How many successful people do you read about or hear about regularly whose ideas were rejected? They did not quit. They simply invested in themselves or took their ideas elsewhere and produced successful results. Look at it this way: Man's rejection could very well be heaven's protection. What another man considers trash could be your treasure. In other words, do not throw your ideas away because someone else did not see their value. What was overlooked or rejected by some could very well be the thing that leads to a promotion. You are perhaps the change agent needed for some organization that's looking to implement those ideas. They simply need someone with your expertise and experience.

You may not see the change immediately and find yourself becoming frustrated by it. Take time to refocus and look at it from another angle. While you are working to gain additional skills that will assist in your efforts to implement change in your current position, you are also being equipped and prepared for your next position.

*Your life matters
even in the workplace.
Make it count!*

Conclusion

At The End of The Day

Making life happen in the workplace is all about doing what is necessary to enjoy your career and workplace environment. The way you think has a direct impact on the way you feel. If you do not believe it, take note of the next time you wake up in the morning. If you think of how much you're not ready to get up and complain about having to do so, your body will respond by becoming too fatigued to get out of bed. If you are excited about your day, your body will respond to that as well.

Many have gotten into the habit of complaining. It has been said that it takes 21 days to break a habit. Therefore, the art of being positive requires practice. It must be an intentional act. When put into action on a daily basis, the change will become evident. When it's practiced long enough it will become a natural part of you.

It is very easy to complain about your situation as we often do in the workplace. The question is: what are you willing to do to change it? Don't be fooled! You do have options. Whether or not you choose to take advantage of those options and the opportunities presented to you is solely up to you. One thing is certain: Until the pain of staying the same outweighs the pain to change, more than likely you won't!

Everything in life begins and ends with a decision. You are in control, whether you feel like you are or not. The thing you must understand is that you are in control of you. Your supervisors and managers may be in control of telling you how to do your job, but they do not get to control how you feel about doing your job.

At the end of the day, you are responsible for your own happiness. You have to make the decision to not allow anything or anyone to disrupt your day and put you in a bad mood. This is not to say that you will not have moments. As discussed in the previous section on low morale, you will indeed have moments because you are human. The key is not allowing those moments to control and cause you to respond in a negative manner. Do not give anyone ammunition to use against you that will discredit or disqualify you.

Do not expect anyone to believe in you if you are not willing to believe in yourself. Do not expect anyone to do for you what you are not willing to do for yourself. You are accountable for your happiness and successes. What changes are you willing to make when it comes to your career and workplace environment? You may not be able to change the culture of the place, but you are able to change the way you deal with the culture while you are in the place.

Learning to change negative thoughts and behaviors into positive ones is a mastery that requires focus and mental practice.

Transforming the way we think is a persistent process. We can change our minds about a situation, but if we do not pursue the change and retrain our thoughts, our efforts will be in vain. We will only revert to old patterns of thinking because it has become comfortably familiar, even though it is not working. It's like a bone that healed improperly after being broken. It must be broken again and held in place with a hard (persistent) cast in order for it to form properly. This is the same process we must take to retrain our minds to focus on the positive in every situation.

Thought patterns must be broken, reshaped, and retrained. Holding positive thoughts in position and retraining the brain to think differently requires daily effort. After a while, it will no longer be a struggle. Positive thinking will become more natural requiring less effort. You will begin to notice that even though your workplace situations have not changed, your feelings about the situation have changed.

Places of frustration and discomfort are identifiers to unfortified places. If we learn to look at them as such, we can embrace them more freely and build endurance muscles. The tips and tools found here are not to diminish your feelings or experiences. They are designed to give you an outlet and provide you with an alternative perspective.

The workplace really can be an enjoyable experience. You may not be able to make an immediate change regarding your workplace situation, but the knowledge gained from those lessons become transferable skills which are quite valuable. The wisdom gained through every workplace situation empowers your journey should you choose to allow them to do so. Keep in mind, it's all about perspective and changing the way you look, think, and feel about your place(s) of employment. When you change your perspective, you change your world.

*Everything begins and ends with a decision.
Change the way you think,
You will change your life!*

About the Author

Passionate and driven are words that describe Veronica. Believing that whatever you do, you should be a specialist at it; she holds a Bachelor of Arts degree in Public Administration from Shaw University and a Master of Education degree in Training & Development from North Carolina State University. She often states that training is a part of her DNA and believes everyone is born with a purpose. Unfortunately, many never realize that purpose. Therefore, she is one who encourages individuals to pursue and conquer.

On occasion, it takes another person to help individuals see what they may not be able to see in themselves. Veronica is known for her ability to ignite enthusiasm while motivating individuals who simply need direction, insight, or that extra push toward transformation and accomplishing their goals. Such keen insight allows her to empower both young and old to uncover hidden talents, discover additional abilities and develop areas of untapped potential within themselves.

In her role as a Trainer, Motivational Speaker, Transformational Coach, and Ordained Minister, she is known for her tenacious "Making Life Happen" leadership style. Her unique approach to training allows her to reach a broad audience. She specializes in the areas of workforce development and educational training that encourages professional growth, personal development that promotes relational, mental and emotional growth, and ministry training to enhance spiritual growth. This technique coupled with her hands-on approach to training & development helps to bring awareness and increased confidence that unlocks potential to execute gifts and talents effectively. She believes you are never too old to dream. If you can dream it, you can be it. Her ability to motivate and ignite enthusiasm empowers individuals to passionately pursue and obtain their goals that transform dreams into reality.

Ways to Connect

Life is a gift that is meant to be enjoyed, but we cannot sit around simply existing and waiting on it to happen. We must pursue our desires and MAKE LIFE HAPPEN. Everyone has an assigned destiny, but it will require work in order to reach it.

Understanding how to obtain results requires the ability to see beyond current conditions and positions. Sometimes it takes others to help us see what we cannot see within ourselves. "VeronicaTrains" functions to educate, motivate, and empower individuals and their ideas with spiritual, emotional, and mental tools used to transform dreams into reality.

Available for workshops, conferences, seminars and training events upon request. For more information and to inquire about scheduling, please visit:

www.veronicatrains.com

Making Life Happen on a Budget

Stay trendy without spending your entire paycheck. Have you been wanting to travel but can't seem to find the money to make it happen? Getting what you want does not have to be expensive. You only have to know how to be skillful in your purchasing decisions. It is possible to enjoy yourself and make life happen without depleting your bank account.

Making Life Happen in the Workplace Training Manual

Mastering the art of making the best of workplace experiences often requires a change of focus. Learning to control emotions and make better decisions is reflected in the way we think, act and respond. This training will empower individuals to embrace their workplace environments, navigate through difficult situations, and have a more enjoyable work life.

"Making Life Happen"

is a series of books and materials designed to help you to live your best life. They are designed to train you to think, act and respond differently for more optimized results.

Stay tuned for more to come.

Copyright © 2019
Veronica G. Burnette
All Rights Reserved

www.ingramcontent.com/pod-product-compliance
Lightning Source LLC
Chambersburg PA
CBHW060819050426
42449CB00008B/1741